STAYING on the PATH

Also by Dr. Wayne W. Dyer

BOOKS

Being in Balance
Change Your Thoughts—Change Your Life
Excuses Begone!
Inspiration
Living the Wisdom of the Tao
Manifest Your Destiny
No More Holiday Blues
The Power of Intention (also available in a CD program, card deck, and calendar)
A Promise Is a Promise
Pulling Your Own Strings
Real Magic
The Shift
The Sky's the Limit
10 Secrets for Success and Inner Peace
There Is a Spiritual Solution to Every Problem
What Do You Really Want for Your Children?
Wisdom of the Ages
Wishes Fulfilled
You'll See It When You Believe It
Your Erroneous Zones
Your Sacred Self

Please visit Hay House USA: **www.hayhouse.com®;** Hay House Australia:
www.hayhouse.com.au; Hay House UK: **www.hayhouse.co.uk;**
Hay House South Africa: **www.hayhouse.co.za;** Hay House India:
www.hayhouse.co.in

STAYING on the PATH

Dr. Wayne W. Dyer

HAY HOUSE, INC.
Carlsbad, California • New York City
London • Sydney • Johannesburg
Vancouver • Hong Kong • New Delhi

Published and distributed in the United States by: Hay House, Inc.:
www.hayhouse.com • *Published and distributed in Australia by:* Hay House Australia
Pty. Ltd.: www.hayhouse.com.au • *Published and distributed in the United Kingdom
by:* Hay House UK, Ltd.: www.hayhouse.co.uk • *Published and distributed in the
Republic of South Africa by:* Hay House SA (Pty), Ltd.: www.hayhouse.co.za •
Distributed in Canada by: Raincoast: www.raincoast.com • *Published in India by:* Hay
House Publishers India: www.hayhouse.co.in

Editorial supervision: Jill Kramer   *Design:* Summer McStravick

Library of Congress Control Number: 2003113242

ISBN 13: 978-1-4019-0349-7
ISBN 10: 1-4019-0349-5

17 16 15 14 13 12 11
1st printing, August 2004

Printed in the USA

For my mother, Hazel Irene Dyer, who used
her magnificent vision and intention to clear
so many obstacles from her own path—I love you.

A Few Words from Dr. Wayne W. Dyer

I've created this book for those of you who are already on the path—as well as those of you who are just trying to get there. My observations may strike a chord in your life at present, or you might find that they come in handy a little way down the line. Whatever the case, just by picking up this book, you're already making headway on your own particular course.

May your journey be a safe and loving one.

All of us are on our own paths, doing exactly what we know how to do at the moment, given the conditions of our lives.

The measure of
your life will not
be in what you
accumulate, but in
what you give away.

The secret of abundance is to stop focusing
on what you do not have, and shift your
consciousness to an appreciation for all
that you are and all that you *do* have.

Practice being in the world, but not of the world—
learn to ignore how things outside of you are going,
and know that higher awareness is
truly a disappearing act.

Send out love and harmony,
put your mind and body in a
peaceful place, and then
allow the universe to work
in the perfect way that it
knows how.

I don't have to be directed by anything outside of myself. God is within me, and the infinite and divine power that gives me sustenance as a human being is always there.

You can never
get enough of what
you don't want.

You can't go around being
what everyone expects you
to be, living your life through
other people's rules, and be
happy and have inner peace.

The only antidote to anger is to eliminate the internal sentences, "If only you were more like I am," and "If only the world were not the way it is."

Meditation gives you
an opportunity to come
to know your invisible
self. It will shatter
the illusion of your
separateness.

Did you ever notice how difficult it is to argue with someone who's not obsessed with being right?

Your suffering comes from needing things to be different. When you stop that, your suffering stops. You can want things, but it is the needing that must go.

Life is an attitude.
It's what you choose
to believe, always.

When my daughter Tracy came home in
the second grade and said, "Billy doesn't like
me, Billy doesn't like me," I responded,
"Do *you* like you?" Tracy said, "Yes."
Then I replied, "Well, that's all you've got."
You see, even at seven years of age,
a person shouldn't get the idea that
anyone else's reactions to you need
to get you down in any way.

Why not think about some things you've never done before and do them simply because you've never done them and for no other reason?

A sense of purpose isn´t something that you find; it´s something that you are. Truth isn´t something that you look for; it´s something that you live.

Nothing out there is bad unless you believe that it is.

Your body is the garage
where you park your soul.

Life is never boring,
but some people choose to be
bored . . . boredom is a choice.

If you choose not to respect your sense of justice, you choose not to respect yourself, and you will soon end up wondering how much your life is really worth.

If you want to be confident but don't normally act that way, then today, just this once, act in the physical world the way you believe a confident person would.

Anything that keeps
you from growing is
never worth defending.

Your reputation is in the hands of others. That's what a reputation is. You can't control that. The only thing you can control is your character.

There are two ways to look at virtually anything. One is the violent way, and one is the peaceful way. It's the yin and yang of the universe.

Your opinions are trivial,
but your commitments to them make
all the difference in the world.

When you live on a round planet,
there's no choosing sides.

The total being called
human being cannot function
harmoniously when its
components are in conflict.

My belief about compassion is summed up by the old saying, "Give a man a fish and he eats for a day; *teach* a man to fish and he eats for a lifetime."

If enough of us shied away from conflict and confrontation, just imagine how much war we could eliminate.

You have a very powerful mind that can make anything happen as long as you keep yourself centered.

Creativity means believing
that you have greatness.

The highest form of
ignorance is to reject something
you know nothing about.

You were a winner from the
moment you were born. There were
several hundred billion sperm in one glob
chasing this one egg. They were all in a race.
The prize was this egg, and they were all swimming
as fast as they could. There were billions
of them, and you won. You won the
first race you were ever in.

A non-doer is very often a critic—
that is, someone who sits back
and watches doers, and then waxes
philosophically about how the
doers are doing. It's easy to be a
critic, but being a doer requires
effort, risk, and change.

Death is merely a form of transformation.
Imagine what our planet would be like
without it. It's like taking off a
worn-out garment.

As long as you stay where you are and tell yourself you have to do it because you've always done it, the only payoff you get is to defend your misery.

Once you become
detached from things,
they don't own you any longer.

Reexamine the sentence,
"Just do your best."
I would substitute it with,
"Just do."

There is no *way*
to enlightenment.
Enlightenment is the way.
It's a principle of living
rather than seeking.

Every moment that you spend upset,
in despair, in anguish, angry, or hurt
because of the behavior of anybody
else is a moment in which you've
given up control of your life.

"It's the space between the bars that holds the tiger," as they say in Zen, and it's the silence between the notes that makes the music.

Throughout life,
the two most futile emotions
are guilt for what *has been*
done and worry about what
might be done.

Failure is an editorial judgment imposed by others.

Everything your form needs to house this soul that you are wears out and changes and dies, but the divine, formless you never dies.

Your own expectations are the key to
the whole business of mental health.
If you expect to be happy, healthy,
and fulfilled in life, then that's where
you'll place your attention, and that's
what you will manifest.

True inner serenity
will always elude those
who sit in judgment,
since they use up their
life energy in anger
at what is.

If you're a person who lives one way,
but who says you're going to live
another way in the future,
those proclamations are empty.

People who have behaved
toward you in any way that
you find disagreeable truly
don't know what they've done
to you because they're living
out of their separateness.

How old would you be if you didn't
know how old you are?

Being *against* anything
weakens you, while being
for something empowers you.

Take the time to
observe animals.
What you learn will
enrich your life.

There's no lack of opportunity to make a living at what you love. There's only a lack of resolve to make it happen.

Be consistently aware of the need to serve God and to serve others in any and all of your actions. That is the way of the miracle worker.

Everything we fight only weakens us and hinders our ability to see the opportunity in the obstacle.

Human beings who do damage or inflict pain on anybody else are far greater victims than those they victimize, and must answer to a law of the universe for all those things.

Guilt takes place in the present moment, as does everything. It's a way of using up the present moment to be consumed with something that has already happened, over which you have no control.

The antecedent to
every action is a thought.

Habits are changed by practicing
new behavior, and this is true for
mental habits as well.

The people who get the most respect
in this world are those who are the straightest,
even though they often take the most abuse.

The first step to healing anything in your life is to
understand that whatever disease process is
going on within you is something you carry around.
You own it all. It's all yours.

You're the creator
of your thoughts, which means
that in some metaphysical way,
you're the creator of your life.

It isn't the world that makes you unhappy, or the way people are in the world. It's how you process the people and events of the world.

Instead of judging others as people who ought to behave in certain ways, see them as reflecting a part of you, and ask yourself what it is you're ready to learn from them.

Create an inner harmony where your loving soul guides your physical behavior, rather than having your soul always come in second place.

Live the Ten Commandments.

The more you have a harmonious, loving, accepting approach, the more you'll see the rest of the pieces all fitting nicely together.

One of the most responsible things you can do as an adult is to become more of a child.

Honor this incarnation
and be fully alive.

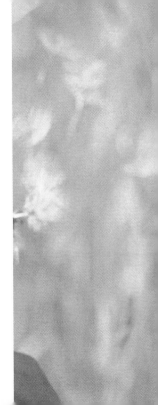

Just because a person is young or small does not make him or her incomplete. The truth is that we are complete at all moments in our life.

Live . . . be you . . . enjoy . . . love.

To change yourself, look at what you
fear and what you hate. Start there.

Your circumstances don't determine what your life will be, they reveal what kinds of images you've chosen up till now.

There are limits to material growth, but there are no limits to inner enlightenment.

A special kind of freedom is available to you if you're willing to take the risks involved in getting it: the freedom to wander where you will about life's terrain, to make all your own choices.

Within you is the kingdom
of serenity that can create
all of the prosperity that
you could ever want.

When you know that you're in charge of your intentions, then you'll come to know that you're in charge of your entire world.

Jealousy is really a demand that someone love you in a certain way, and you saying, "It isn't fair" when they don't.
It comes from a lack of self-confidence.

If you refuse to change your job (if you don't like it), the only sensible thing you can do is practice loving it every day.

Send out anger and impatience, and that's what you'll get. Send out love, and you'll get back love.

You can set yourself
up to be sick, or you can
choose to be well.

The more you extend kindness to yourself, the more it will become your automatic response to others.

Your body is perfect. It knows how to do all the things that bodies are capable of doing. It knows how to walk, sweat, sleep, be hungry, cry . . . it's also a very good learner. You can teach it to swim, drive a car, write a letter, play a guitar, cut a diamond, or climb a mountain.

Observe yourself and others in this
nutty world, and then decide whether
to carry around anger or to develop a sense
of humor that will give you and others one of
the most priceless gifts of all—laughter.

No one, regardless of how much he or she wishes it, can put understanding into another human being. Understanding can only come from doing.

I can assure you that once you no longer need the lessons in your life that unpleasant events offer you, you will no longer experience these events.

Those who seem to cause you the most anguish are those who remind you of what is either lacking or wanting in yourself.

Your joy is divine and so is your suffering. There's so much to be learned from both.

When you argue
for your limitations,
all you get are
your limitations.

A lot of people have bumper stickers that say, "This is the first day of the rest of my life." I prefer to think, "This is the last day of my life, and I'm going to live it as if I don't have any more."

You're always alone, but
you're only lonely if you
don't like the person
you're alone with.

You have to risk some feelings
of insecurity if you're ever going
to learn to walk a tightrope,
water-ski, become a writer,
start a new business, try out a
new recipe, or do anything
that requires learning.

The "un" in
unconditional
means not judging.

We can never become awakened or enlightened until we can move beyond form. Every philosopher who ever lived has taught that.

People generally stop having
hurt feelings when they realize
that those feelings can no longer
be used to manipulate you.

You must come in contact with
the empty space that lies within,
not the form that encapsulates it.

Your miracles are an inside job. Go there to create the magic that you seek in your life.

When you think positive, happy, loving thoughts, there's a different chemistry that goes into your body than when you think depressing, negative, anguished thoughts. The way you decide to think has a dramatic effect on your chemistry and on your physiology.

Your right to swing your fist stops
with my right to have my nose
shaped the way I want it.

A flabby lifestyle is inexcusable.
All of your reasons for being out of
shape are nothing but excuses
you make to yourself.

There's not one cell in your body today that was there seven years ago. Yet you can remember being alive seven years ago. How do you account for that?

Looking into the mirror and disliking the self that you take with you everywhere you go is one of the most self-defeating things you can do.

No-limit people are so in charge
that they can trust their instincts,
be childlike, be creative, and do
anything that makes sense to them.

The past is over for all of us.
The future is promised to none of us.
All we get is this one.
That's all we get.

St. Mark said,
"With God, all things are possible."
Now what does that leave out?

Everyone deserves our love,
and until we start thinking that way,
we're always going to have
us versus *them* thinking.

You are in a partnership with all
other human beings, not a
contest to be judged better than
some and worse than others.

Every obstacle that comes along on this planet is either an opportunity to grow and think differently . . . or to use as an excuse to believe that we're stuck.

Life presents itself to you
and asks nothing of you.
You can take life and swim
deliriously through it, or you
can fight it. But when you
elect to spend your time
fighting it, you can't use
the same time to enjoy it.

Each problem is an
opportunity in disguise.

It's not what is available or
unavailable that determines your level
of success and happiness; it's what
you convince yourself is true.

If things aren't working, ask yourself,
"In what way am I creating this? In what
way can I change? What is the lesson?"

Helping somebody else achieve a sense
of purpose is a part of the mission of
what it means to be a parent.

Everything in life is a
paradox. The less you care
whether you get approval,
the more you get.

There's a big difference between not liking someone's behavior and not liking *someone*.

Try to learn from the past,
rather than repeating it and
making references to it all the time.

You can never please everyone.
In fact, if you please 50 percent of the
people, you're doing quite well.

Each experience in your life was absolutely necessary in order to have gotten you to the next place, and the next, up until this very moment.

When the universe is presented
with a problem, does it say,
"I don't know how to deal with this"?
No. The universe is perfect.

The only boundaries we have are in form. There are no obstacles in thought.

Love is forgiving . . .
and love is for giving.

Chasing success is like trying to squeeze
a handful of water. The tighter you squeeze,
the less water you get. With success, when you
chase it, your life becomes the chase, and you
never arrive at a place called *successful*.
You become a victim of wanting more.

Remember what Victor Hugo told us: "Nothing is more powerful than an idea whose time has come."

All of the ``stuff'' in your life has arrived to serve you, rather than to make you a servant of the stuff.

Prejudice means to "pre-judge."
When you do so, you're making a
decision about something before
you have enough data on which
to base a decision.

If you get pushed around,
you've been sending
push-me-around signals.

When you truly know that your life has a grand and heroic mission, you'll realign yourself as a spiritual being.

You leave old habits
behind by starting
out with the thought,
*I release the need
for this in my life.*

A purpose isn't something
that you're going to find.
It's something that will find you.
And it will find you only when
you're ready and not before.

Get your nose out of
everybody else's garden.
Get your own in order,
and stop focusing on
everybody else's.

In any relationship in which two people become one, the end result is two half people.

Risk is only your evaluation of it.

You can reshape your thinking so that you never have to think in negatives again. You and only you choose your thoughts.

Some people believe that they live a life of lack because they're unlucky, instead of realizing that their belief systems are rooted in scarcity thinking.

Only insecure people need security.
Secure people know that there's
no such thing. Security comes from
within, when you know you
can handle anything.

They used to say to scientists, "Do you believe in God?" And the scientist would respond, "No, I'm a scientist." Today, in the 21st century, if you ask a scientist, "Do you believe in God?" the scientist will say, "Of course. I'm a scientist!"

Be patient and loving
with every fearful thought.

When you're at peace with yourself
and you love yourself, it's virtually
impossible for you to do things to
yourself that are destructive.

Self-esteem comes
from the self, not
from acquisitions
and approval.

You cannot always be number one, or always win a contest, or always get the merit badge, or always make the honor roll, but you can always think of yourself as an important, worthwhile person.

Our beliefs about ourselves
are the most telling factors in
determining our level of success
and happiness in life.

Every single condition in your life can
be improved if you learn to be more
effective at visualizing what you want
and having the intention to manifest it.

Individuals who use self-labels
are stating, "I'm a finished product
in this area, and I'm never going to
be any different." If you're a
finished product, all tied up and
put away, you've stopped growing.

Make a personal decision to be in
love with the most beautiful, exciting,
worthy person ever—*you!*

Whenever other people are upset,
always remember that they own the upset,
and that you can refuse to join them.

With everything that has happened to you, you can either feel sorry for yourself, or treat what has happened as a gift. Everything is either an opportunity to grow or an obstacle to keep you from growing. You get to choose.

Buddha said,
"You will not be
punished *for* your
anger. You will
be punished *by*
your anger."

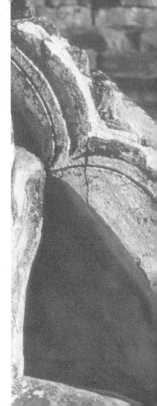

No one can depress you.
No one can make you anxious. No one can hurt
your feelings. No one can make you anything
other than what you allow inside.

Don't equate your self-worth with how well you
do things in life. You aren't what you do. If you
are what you do, then when you don't, you aren't.

You don't have to be a person who's at
the mercy of anyone who chooses to annoy you.

Shy people make shy pictures over and over
in their minds, and until they see themselves
as unafraid, they'll always act on the
pictures they create.

What makes you human is not this form, but the invisible intelligence that suffuses it—mind, spirit, God, whatever you want to call it.

Imagine the word CANCEL being a huge rubber stamp in your mind. Stamp CANCEL on any self-defeating image you place in your head, and begin to think in a self-enhancing way.

Suffering comes from wants.

We become what we think about all day long. The question is, "What do you think about?"

Surrender to a new consciousness,
a thought that whispers, "I can
do this thing in this moment. I will
receive all the help that I need as
long as I stay with this intention
and go within for assistance."

Advance confidently in the
direction of your own dreams to
live the life that you've imagined.
That's when you have success.

There's a rhythm to the universe. When we're able to get quiet enough, we experience how we're a part of that perfect rhythm.

We all have a well of infinite depth
within us that contains more potential
for creativity than we can ever imagine.

You can make your life into a grand, ever-evolving work of art. The key is your thoughts, the wondrous, invisible part of you that is your spiritual soul.

You mustn't attempt
to *will* anything.
You need only be willing.

The use of mental imagery is one of the strongest and most effective strategies for making something happen for you.

When you get enough inner peace
and feel really positive about yourself,
it's almost impossible for you to be controlled
and manipulated by anybody else.

If you find yourself being treated in a way you resent or that turns you into a victim, ask yourself this question: "What have I done to teach this person that this behavior is something I'm willing to tolerate?"

How do you get world peace? You get world peace through inner peace. If you've got a world full of people who have inner peace, then you have a peaceful world.

Everything I ever worried about turned out exactly as it was going to despite my anxious moments to the contrary.

All you need in order
to have total happiness,
fulfillment, and love in your
life you already have right
now, whoever you are,
wherever you are.

The children whom you
admire so much for their ability
to enjoy life aren't foreign
creatures to you. You have one
of those children inside you.

One of the really good exercises for releasing attachments is to go through your garage and your closets and take all the things that your children don't use anymore and give them away. Have your kids participate in this.

Everything that's happening
is supposed to be happening.

Doing what you love is
the cornerstone of having
abundance in your life.

Analyzing is really a violent intellectual act. When you analyze something, you have to break it apart and find every little piece of it.

You control your emotions, so you don't have to explode with anger whenever someone else decides to behave in angry ways.

Loving people live in a loving world.
Hostile people live in a hostile world.
Same world. How come?

You can't be authentic unless
you're following your bliss.

The path to the big picture is different
for everyone, but the understanding
has to be that the big picture is there,
and its availability is there.

Believe it and you'll see it.
Know it and you'll *be* it!

Since your mind is your own private
territory, you can give any new idea a
private audition for a few days.

There are some people who live 70 years, and there are some people who live one year 70 times, repeating what they're doing over and over in the name of the gold watch or whatever.

If you're looking for love,
it will always elude you.
If you're looking for happiness,
it will always elude you. When
you *become* these things, it's all
you will have to give away.

Stop blaming your spouse for your unhappiness, your parents for your lack of motivation, the economy for your social status, the bakery for your excess weight, your childhood for your phobias, and anything else to which you assign blame points. You're the sum total of the choices you've made in your life.

The way you change your
behavior is to look at the source
of strength that you are.

Feelings aren't emotions that happen to you. Feelings are reactions you choose to have, and they show up in your body as physical reactions to your thoughts.

A child is a wonder to behold.

Behavior is a much better barometer
of what you are than words.

If you practice maintaining your composure, and remember that someone else's behavior belongs to that person and cannot upset you unless you allow it to do so, then you will not become an unwilling target.

The only difference
between a flower and
a weed is judgment.

The opposite of courage is not
so much fear as it is conformity.

You cannot always control what
goes on outside, but you can always
control what goes on inside.

Thoughts are ways in which we can make virtually anything happen.

Your form will simply pass along, but you can't kill thought, so you can't kill who you really are.

If you don't have
confidence in yourself,
get off your rear end and do
anything that will make you
feel better about yourself.

If you believe that this book will liberate you, then you're already a victim of your own illusions. You and only you must decide to take these suggestions and turn them into constructive, self-fulfilling behaviors.

The more you let go of people and things, the fewer obstacles you will have on your life's journey.

The most effective weapon you have in banishing neurotic behavior from your life is your own determination.

Schools must become
caring places full of teachers who
understand that teaching students to
love themselves and feel positive
about their natural curiosity ought
to be given as much attention as
geometry and grammar.

Your emotions shouldn't be immobilizing. They shouldn't be defended. They shouldn't keep you from being all that you can be.

These are the good old days.

Enlightened people move away
from conflict and confrontation.

Develop an inner candle flame
that won't flicker even when the
worst situations befall you.

If you believe that feeling bad or worrying long enough will change a past or future event, then you're residing on another planet, with a different reality system.

How harmony gets inside you
is through your own thinking.

When you're told that you have
some kind of physical affliction,
you can either prepare to suffer
or prepare to heal.

If you slip, it doesn't mean you're less valuable. It simply means you have something to learn from slipping.

Fear of failure
becomes fear of success
for those who never
try anything new.

To not forgive is to fail
to understand how the universe
works and how you fit into it.

An invisible intelligence suffuses all form in the universe, and allows flowers to grow and planets to align and the whole thing to exist.

The more you understand yourself as a human being, the more you realize that you can either flow with life or fight it. And every time you fight something, you get weaker.

Enlightened people have perfect love in them just like everyone else does; the only difference is that they have nothing else in them.

The freest people in the world
are those who have inner peace.

Give love and unconditional
acceptance to those you encounter,
and notice what happens.

Guilt is an irresponsible choice. As long as you feel guilty about whatever you've done, then you don't have to do anything to correct it.

Happiness and success are inner processes that we bring to life's undertakings, rather than something we get from "out there."

The body is a great healer.
That magnificent, perfect creation
is capable of healing itself in
many, many instances.

Healthy thinking is a habit,
just like neurotic thinking is a habit.

If you expect to be upset,
then you'll seldom disappoint yourself.

Highly functioning people say,
"Where I am is fine, but I can grow."

Try viewing everyone who
comes into your life as a teacher.

In Zen they say,
"Before enlightenment, chop wood,
carry water. After enlightenment,
chop wood, carry water."
You've got to chop and carry.
That's just part of the human condition.

Anything that bothers you
is only a problem within.
Only you can experience it,
and only you can correct it.

Instead of judging others as people who should be behaving in certain ways, see them as reflecting a part of you, and ask yourself what it is you're ready to learn from them.

It's intelligent to have a plan,
but neurotic to fall in love with it.

Quality rather than appearance . . .
ethics rather than rules . . .
knowledge rather than achievement . . .
integrity rather than domination . . .
serenity rather than acquisitions.

Intention is the energy of
your soul coming into contact
with your physical reality.

Other people are going to be exactly
the way they are, independent of
your opinion of them.

If you want to find a deeper meaning in your life, you can't find it in the opinions or the beliefs that have been handed to you. You have to go to that place within yourself.

Everything in your life is a miracle to be cherished. A grain of sand, a bee on a flower, a sailboat, a cup of coffee, a wet diaper, a caterpillar, are all miracles. When you learn to view life and everything in it as a miracle, you soon see that complaining is a waste of the miracle that you are.

Loving relationships work
because there is no work.

The only limits you have
are the limits you believe.

You're not your form.
You're something much more
magnificent, divine, and grand.

Anytime you get hate, send out love.
Then love will come back,
and you'll be free.

When you no longer need
to learn how to deal with
disharmony in your life,
you'll stop creating it, and
you'll create love and
harmony virtually
everywhere you turn.

Instead of saying,
"Why is this happening to me?
Isn't this awful. Poor me,"
begin to say, "What do I
have to learn from this?"

That we breathe, that we showed up on this planet, that we communicate, is a miracle.

The purpose of Life is to know God.

The difference between being neurotic and being a no-limit person isn't whether someone has problems. Everyone has problems. It's attitude. Do you look for solutions or more problems?

Networking can never fail.
It's so powerful because you just
keep creating more power sources.
It's like geometric progression.

If you can conceive it in your mind,
then it can be brought into
the physical world.

If you work at living your life a
moment—instead of a decade—at a time,
then you can cope with your challenges.

You can attend a beautiful service every
Sunday, and you can practice all kinds of Bible
sayings, and you can label yourself with the
most fantastic tags that you can come up with,
but you won't find your heart in a temple if
you don't have a temple in your heart.

The beggars in the streets of New Delhi, the boat people in Malaysia, the royalty in Buckingham Palace, the factory workers in Detroit, and you (whoever you are) are all equal cells in the body called humanity.

If children are raised in peace, they will not know how to be warlike.

We are all at once teachers and learners in every encounter of our lives.

Every problem you have you experience in your mind. The solution to the problem is in the same place.

Starvation is part of what the universe is about, but so is my desire to change it.

What's over is over. You did what you knew how to do. It wasn't right or wrong or good or bad. It just was. But all you've got is today. You can't have it back.

No one can get
behind your eyeballs
and experience life
the way you do.

The only difference between
ALONE and ALL ONE is one L . . .
and that stands for *love*.

In matters of taste,
you alone are, and
must be, the sole
judge of what
pleases you.

Everything you
"have to have" owns you.

It takes not one drop of sweat
to put off doing something.

When God speaks through your hands and
smiles upon the earth through you because
you're an unconditional giver, a purposeful
being who asks nothing of anyone . . .
prosperity will be your reward.

As you awaken, you go beyond the need to accumulate and perform and achieve. When you go beyond it, you begin to develop an increased susceptibility to the love extended by others as well as the uncontrollable urge to extend it. Love becomes what you are.

The more space you allow and encourage within a relationship, the more the relationship will flourish.

The moments between events are just as livable as the events themselves.

When you have the choice between being right and being kind, just choose kind.

The War on Drugs is never going
to work . . . because it's a war.

If you don't believe that you control
your thoughts, make a list of who does.
Send them to me. I'll treat them all,
and you'll get better.

The entire gamut of human experience
is yours to enjoy once you decide
to venture into territory where
you don't have guarantees.

Security is ugly.
Security is self-defeating.
Security is boring. Security is dull.
What do you want security for?

If you're in a relationship with someone who's treating you in a rude and obnoxious way, you have to say, "What do I think of myself? Why have I allowed this behavior to persist?" And "Am I going to allow it to continue?"

Being self-actualized means
being able to welcome the unknown.

Taking care of yourself is a natural outgrowth of self-love. Have a quiet love affair with yourself.

Once you begin working on your problem areas with small, daily, success-oriented goals for yourself, the problems will disappear.

If you don't love yourself, nobody else will. Not only that, but you won't be good at loving anyone else. Loving starts with the self.

Perhaps the single most outstanding
characteristic of healthy people
is their unhostile sense of humor.

Those who behave in ways
that you dislike are sending
out their disharmony toward
you because that's all they
have to give away. Hating
them is akin to hating moss
for growing on the tree.

You don't need to let anyone
into your life unless they come
in with love and harmony.

One of the highest places you can
get to is to be independent of the
good opinions of other people.

You're doomed to make choices.
This is life's greatest paradox.

Once you know that what you think
about expands, you start getting really
careful about what you think about.

If you depend on others
for your value, it is
"other-worth,"
not "self-worth."

In Western civilization, we're accustomed to believing that what we produce and what we get for ourselves is a measure of who we are, when, in fact, that's a spiritual dead end.

When you're ready, whatever you need to be transformed will be there.

When you're just like everyone else in the world, you have to ask yourself, "What do I have to offer?"

Happiness, fulfillment, and purpose
in life are all inner concepts.
If you don't have inner peace and
serenity, then you have nothing.

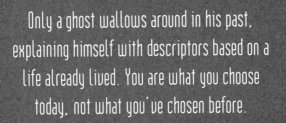

Only a ghost wallows around in his past, explaining himself with descriptors based on a life already lived. You are what you choose today, not what you've chosen before.

A successful person isn't
someone who makes a lot of money.
A successful person brings success to
everything that he or she does, and
money is one of the payoffs.

Your ability to be a winner 100 percent of the time is based upon giving up the notion that losing at anything is equivalent to being a loser.

Our days are the
precious currency of our lives.

If you're suffering in your life
right now, I can guarantee that
you're somehow attached to
how things *should* be going.

The more you work at just being yourself,
the more likely you'll feel purposeful
and significant in your life.

The universal principles will never show up in
your life until you know they're there. When you
believe in them, you'll see them everywhere.

You don't get abused because there are a lot of abusers out there. You get abused because you send out signals that say, "Abuse me. I'll take that."

What you have to
learn to do is to fall in
love with what you do and
then sell that love.

You can spend the rest of your life,
beginning right now, worrying about
the future—and no amount of your
worry will change a thing.

You are whole.
You are complete.
You are total in every
moment that you're alive.

Abundance is about looking at life
and knowing that we have everything
we need for complete happiness,
and then being able to celebrate each
and every moment of life.

What distinguishes
what's alive from
what's dead is
growth, be it in
plants or in you.

To enter the world of real magic,
you must enter the dimension
of spirituality.

There's no anger in the world.
There are only angry thoughts.

Did you ever notice that
some people never have enough,
and other people always have enough?

The next time you get nervous
about others' opinions,
look them mentally in the eye
and say, "What you think of me
is none of my business."

The winning attitude is one that allows you to think of yourself as a winner all the time while still giving yourself room to grow.

People need to be right. If you can
remove that issue from your life,
you'll save yourself lots of suffering.

Be a student. Stay open and willing
to learn from everyone and anyone.
Being a student means you have
room for new input.

You can't kill thought. It's eternal.

You don't have to continue to
behave the way you've behaved just
because you always have.

Even in a prison, your corner of freedom is how you choose to think. No one can ever take that away!

If you think of yourself as an important person, you won´t allow yourself to be overweight or suffer from any eating disorder.

Somehow we've got this
notion that life is a dress rehearsal.
It isn't. This is it!

You can have no inner peace
as long as the controls of your life
are located outside yourself.

If you believe it will work out,
you'll see opportunities. If you believe
it won't, you'll see obstacles.

Whenever you're tempted to give less,
try giving a little extra instead.

Send all your enemies love. It's easy
to love some people. The true test is to
love someone who's hard to love.

Forgiveness is the most powerful thing you can do to get on the spiritual path. If you can't do it, you can forget about getting to higher levels of awareness and creating real magic in your life.

Babe Ruth struck out more than anybody in the history of baseball the year he hit 60 home runs. Do you want to hit home runs? You'd better be willing to strike out a lot.

Healthy habits are learned in the same way as unhealthy ones—through practice.

Guilt means that you use up your present moments being immobilized as a result of past behavior.

Listen to your body, and it
will tell you what you need to know.

A woman asked me one time, "What are
the blocks to my happiness?" I said,
"The belief that you have blocks."

Once people know that you're intimidated by their anger, they'll use it to victimize you whenever it will work.

If you take two sentences out of your life: "I'm tired," and "I don't feel well," you will have cured about 50 percent of your fatigue and illness.

You become what you think about all day long, and those days become your lifetime.

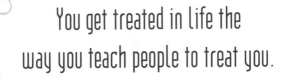

You get treated in life the
way you teach people to treat you.

Give up the want; know that you don't need one more thing to make yourself complete, and then watch all those external things become less and less significant in your heart.

Shift your focus from
What's in it for me?
to *How may I serve?*

If you're pessimistic about anything or have any hatred or dislike in you, that is the place to go to work. That's the evidence that you aren't living with a temple in your heart.

The key to being effective and awake in our lives is to be students rather than teachers.

Great things have no fear of time.

To live your life in the way you choose, you have to be a bit rebellious. You have to be willing to stand up for yourself.

Inner development is just as important
as outer physical development.

―――――⟡―――――

Being relaxed, at peace with yourself,
confident, emotionally neutral, loose, and
free-floating—these are the keys to successful
performance in almost everything.

The only difference between someone who's beautiful and unattractive is a judgment. There's nobody in the world who's unattractive. Unattractive is just what people decide to believe.

Detachment is one of
life's great lessons for
those on the path to
enlightenment.

Examine the labels you
apply to yourself. Every single
label is a boundary or a limit
of one kind or another.

Your joy is divine and
so is your suffering.
There's so much to be
learned from both.

Your lifetime in form is to be honored
and celebrated. Go beyond your
enslavement and live fully in
the now, the only time you have.

The elevator to
success is out of order
today. You're going
to have to take the
stairway, one step
at a time.

If 90 percent of doctors
don't believe in the mind-body
connection, how do they
wiggle their toes?

Neurotics are looking for problems.
They want things to get worse.
They want to be right.

The NOW is a magical place where you're uniquely capable of being so involved that there's no room for any unhappy or debilitating thoughts.

You're always a valuable, worthwhile human being, not because anybody else says so, not because you're successful, not because you make a lot of money, but because you decide to know it.

If you think that the solution is outside of yourself, but the problem is *inside* of yourself, then you're living an illusion. The fact is that every problem is in your mind, and so is every solution.

The way to oneness seems to be through
the path of inner harmony. The way to inner
harmony is through thought.

Children need to know that the words
"It's impossible" are not a part of your vocabulary
and that you're a supporter of their dreams.

Everything that happens to
us has a blessing built into it.

Inner perfection is there
for each one of us to recapture.

More is less. For me, having more means having to insure it, protect it, polish it, worry about it, brag about it, price it, maybe sell it for a profit, and on and on.

The only way you'll ever quit smoking is to not put cigarettes in your mouth one day at a time.

You overcome old habits
by leaving them behind.

When you come to another with love in your heart, asking nothing, only offering that love, you create miraculous relationships.

The state of your life is nothing more
than a reflection of your state of mind.

As long as you're willing to stay as you are
or to stay only with the familiar and not take
risks and try out new things, then it is,
by definition, impossible to grow.

Rather than fretting about your past or future
relationship with your parents, try to be as pleasing
and interested in them as you can—today!

The next time you're contemplating a decision in which you're debating whether or not to take charge of yourself or to make your own choices, ask yourself an important question: "How long am I going to be dead?"

It's never
too late to have a
happy childhood.

If you don't take time for your health now,
then you will have to take time later.

When you *know* rather than *doubt,*
you'll discover the necessary
ability to carry out your purpose.

Fear itself doesn't exist in the world. There are only fearful thoughts and avoidance behaviors.

You must become the producer, director, and actor in the unfolding story of your life.

Most people are searching for
happiness. They're looking for it.
They're trying to find it in someone
or something outside of themselves.
That's a fundamental mistake.
Happiness is something that
you are, and it comes from
the way that you think.

Your love is located within you.
It's yours to nurture and savor. It's yours
to give in any way you choose. This is true
for others as well: If someone you love
fails to return the love the way you would like
it returned, that's the other person's choice.
It doesn't at all detract from *your* love.

Giving love to others is directly related to how much love you have for yourself.

Whatever is going on inside of you is up to you. You own it all. It's yours.

You have the power to become
anything you want to.
Set your expectations for yourself,
and know that you'll become
whatever you think about.

We're all on the same path.
We're just on different places
along that path.

When the holiday season comes along, put a sign on your bathroom mirror that says very emphatically: NO ONE IS GOING TO RUIN THIS SEASON FOR ME . . . ESPECIALLY YOURS TRULY!

Make cooperation and service
the rule in all your business dealings.

There is no *path* to success;
success is an inner attitude that
we bring to our endeavors.

The person looking back at you
in the mirror is the one you
have to answer to every day.

Being a victim is a habit.

You go out into the world,
and you are who you choose to be,
and you know that some of the people
will like it and others won't.

The universe works on many principles that are beyond our control. They work independent of our opinion about them and work even if we don't understand them.

When you become immobilized by what anybody else thinks of you, what you're saying is: "Your opinion of me is more important than my own opinion of myself."

Worry is a means of using up the present moment in being consumed about something in the future, over which you have no control.

If others hurt you,
let the injury go.
This is your test.
If you let it go,
you'll find serenity.

Instead of getting mad at the world for the way that it is, let's accept it and do what we can to improve it.

If you build a house that has
as its foundation only one
support system and that
particular support collapses,
your entire house will topple.

The only limitations you have to magical relationships are those you've imposed upon yourself.

You are unique in all the world.

If you *are* love, and you *live* love,
and you send it out, there will be
so much love in your life that you
won't know what to do with it.

About the Author

Affectionately called the "father of motivation" by his fans, **Dr. Wayne W. Dyer** was an internationally renowned author, speaker, and pioneer in the field of self-development. Over the four decades of his career, he wrote more than 40 books (21 of which became *New York Times* bestsellers), created numerous audio programs and videos, and appeared on thousands of television and radio shows. His books *Manifest Your Destiny, Wisdom of the Ages, There's a Spiritual Solution to Every Problem,* and the *New York Times* bestsellers *10 Secrets for Success and Inner Peace, The Power of Intention, Inspiration, Change Your Thoughts–Change Your Life, Excuses Begone!, Wishes Fulfilled,* and *I Can See Clearly Now* were all featured as National Public Television specials.

Wayne held a doctorate in educational counseling from Wayne State University, had been an associate professor at St. John's University in New York, and honored a lifetime commitment to learning and finding the Higher Self. In 2015, he left his body, returning to Infinite Source to embark on his next adventure.

Website: www.DrWayneDyer.com

Hay House Lifestyles Titles of Related Interest

Empowerment Cards (a 50-card deck), by Tavis Smiley

Everyday Positive Thinking, by Louise L. Hay

Feng Shui Dos & Taboos for Health and Well-being,
by Angi Ma Wong

Meditations, by Sylvia Browne

Simple Things, by Jim Brickman, with Cindy Pearlman

Wisdom of the Heart, by Alan Cohen

All of the above are available at your local bookstore,
or may be ordered through Hay House.

We hope you enjoyed this Hay House Lifestyles book.
If you would like to receive our online catalog featuring
additional Hay House books and products, or if you would like
information about the Hay Foundation, please contact:

Hay House, Inc.
P.O. Box 5100
Carlsbad, CA 92018-5100

(760) 431-7695 or **(800) 654-5126**
(760) 431-6948 (fax) or **(800) 650-5115 (fax)**
www.hayhouse.com® • **www.hayfoundation.org**

Published and distributed in Australia by:
Hay House Australia Pty. Ltd., 18/36 Ralph St., Alexandria NSW 2015 •
Phone: 6129669-4299 • *Fax:* 612-9669-4144 • www.hayhouse.com.au

Published and distributed in the United Kingdom by:
Hay House UK, Ltd., Astley House, 33 Notting Hill Gate, London W11 3JQ
Phone: 44-20-3675-2450 • *Fax:* 44-20-3675-2451 • www.hayhouse.co.uk

Published and distributed in the Republic of South Africa by:
Hay House SA (Pty), Ltd., P.O. Box 990, Witkoppen 2068 •
Phone/Fax: 27-11-467-8904 • info@hayhouse.co.za
www.hayhouse.co.za

Published in India by: Hay House Publishers India, Muskaan Complex, Plot No. 3, B-2, Vasant Kunj, New Delhi 110 070 • **Phone:** 91-11-4176-1620 • **Fax:** 91-11-4176-1630 • www.hayhouse.co.in

Distributed in Canada by: Raincoast, 9050 Shaughnessy St., Vancouver, B.C. V6P 6E5 • **Phone:** (604) 323-7100 • **Fax:** (604) 323-2600 • www.raincoast.com

Take Your Soul on a Vacation

Visit **www.HealYourLife.com**® to regroup, recharge, and reconnect with your own magnificence.
Featuring blogs, mind-body-spirit news, and life-changing wisdom from Louise Hay and friends.

Visit **www.HealYourLife.com** today!